A PLUCKED ZITHER

A PLUCKED ZITHER

poems

~

Phuong T. Vuong

2021
Benjamin Saltman
Poetry Award

Red Hen Press | *Pasadena, CA*

Book design by Mark E. Cull

Library of Congress Cataloging-in-Publication Data

Names: Vuong, Phuong T., 1987– author.
Title: A plucked zither: poems / Phuong T. Vuong.
Description: First edition. | Pasadena, CA: Red Hen Press, [2023]
Identifiers: LCCN 2022044671 (print) | LCCN 2022044672 (ebook) | ISBN
    9781636280950 (paperback) | ISBN 9781636280967 (ebook)
Subjects: LCGFT: Poetry.
Classification: LCC PS3622.U97 P59 2023 (print) | LCC PS3622.U97 (ebook)
  | DDC 811/.6—dc23/eng/20220915
LC record available at https://lccn.loc.gov/2022044671
LC ebook record available at https://lccn.loc.gov/2022044672

Publication of this book has been made possible in part through the generous financial sup-
port of Ann Beman.

The National Endowment for the Arts, the Los Angeles County Arts Commission, the Ahman-
son Foundation, the Dwight Stuart Youth Fund, the Max Factor Family Foundation, the Pasadena
Tournament of Roses Foundation, the Pasadena Arts & Culture Commission and the City of Pasa-
dena Cultural Affairs Division, the City of Los Angeles Department of Cultural Affairs, the Audrey
& Sydney Irmas Charitable Foundation, the Meta & George Rosenberg Foundation, the Albert and
Elaine Borchard Foundation, the Adams Family Foundation, Amazon Literary Partnership, the
Sam Francis Foundation, and the Mara W. Breech Foundation partially support Red Hen Press.

First Edition
Published by Red Hen Press
www.redhen.org

Acknowledgments

Many thanks to the editors and readers of the journals where these poems originally appeared.

American Poetry Review: "Trịnh Công Sơn's Children," "Traversence"; *Apogee*: "Home-cooking"; *Black Warrior Review*: "Natural Melancholia"; *Crazyhorse*: "In My Afterlife, I Am Brightest," "A Repeating Distance"; *Duende*: "Country of Origin"; *Hayden's Ferry Review*: "If Language is a Metaphor Between Sound and Meaning," "Grandmother Says: New Theorems"; *Juked*: "Exception," "Bà Nội, She Will Rest at Sea"; *The Margins* (Asian American Writers' Workshop): "Immigrant's Lament," "Migration's Undoing"; *Moonroot Zine*: "Ode to Sweet Potato Greens"; *Prairie Schooner*: "This is the Dream"; *Puerto del Sol*: "Familiar Logic," "In the Canals of Thought," "Legacy / Inheritance / Fortune / Gia tài"; *Wildness*: "Reacquaintances."

For my grandparents whom I get to know, after. I trace a line to you.

Thank you to my parents who make music in their own ways. It reverberates. Thank you for sharing Trịnh Công Sơn's work with me.

Thank you to Red Hen Press for this opportunity and for bringing my book to life. Thank you, Major Jackson, for selecting my manuscript for the Benjamin Saltman Poetry Award. An honor to be mentioned in your company! Thank you Jessica TranVo for sharing your gorgeous artwork for the cover.

Thank you to my friends, MFA colleagues, and professors at CU Boulder, especially Ruth Ellen Kocher, Khadijah Queen, Julie Carr, Matthieu LeGrenade Nilufar Karimi, Jim Miranda, Rushi Vyas. Many of these poems started in your company and improved with your comments and guidance. Professors Cheryl Higashida and Seema Sohi, so much gratitude for all I have learned with you and for your ongoing mentorship.

Thank you to my current department, PhD cohort, and the MFA students at UCSD for your support and encouragement, in particular my committee: Shelley Streeby, Erin Suzuki, Hoang Tan Nguyen, Katie Walkiewicz, Yến Lê Espiritu. Thank you to Kazim Ali, Lily Hoàng, Brandon Som for the warm welcome and to Teo Rivera-Dundas and Vyxz Vasquez, who share the writing life.

To writing friends and community near and far, from shenanigans at VONA to Tin House: Jada Reneé Allen, Amy M. Alvarez, Destiny O. Birdsong, Isabella Borgenson, Ashley Davis, Sonia Guiñansaca, Rezina Habtemariam, Alice Hall, feí hernández, Luz Jiménez, Caits Meissner, Anis Mojgani, Madeleine Mori, Ximena Serrano-Keogh, Keith S. Wilson, Tatiana Zamir. To poets and teachers, Ruth Forman, Patricia Smith, and Shane McCrae, how fortunate I have been to learn from you! To Vickie Vértiz, Kenji C. Liu, Muriel Leung, and Jade Cho, who live the word "community." To the 30x30 crew: TK Lê, Narinda Heng, Tina Zafreen Alam, Jubi Arriola-Headley, Ami Patel, Laura Villarreal, and others for helping the words come. I appreciate the She Who Has No

Masters Collective for conversations and creative propulsion: Dao Strom, Hoa Nguyen, Diana Khoi Nguyen, Vi Khi Nao, Anh-Hoa Thi Nguyen, Nhã Thuyên, Barbara Tran, and others I hope to meet soon.

Thank you to my friends—artists, scholars, brilliant in their own right—for years and years of love and support: Tierra Allen, Denicia Cadena, Paige Chung, Rocio Cisneros, mai c. doan, José Antonio Galloso, Anthony A. Jack, Esther Kang, Shruti Kaul, Ajayi Lawrence, Claudia Leung, Lau Malaver, Jennifer Nguyen, võ hài, Tracy Wu, Jackie Zaneri, Megan Zapanta. Thank you to Maya Misra, Stacey Uy, and many others at Asian Solidarity Collective for reorienting me into being-with. Nothing—not even writing—is done alone.

Contents

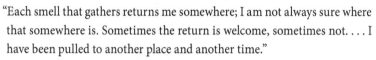

"Each smell that gathers returns me somewhere; I am not always sure where that somewhere is. Sometimes the return is welcome, sometimes not. . . . I have been pulled to another place and another time."

—Sara Ahmed

"To be in transit is to be active presence in a world of relational movements and countermovements. To be in transit is to exist relationally, multiply."

—Jodi Byrd

Country of Origin

after Safia Elhillo

> *country: from Latin roots meaning, "against, opposite"*
> *and "(land) lying opposite"*
> —Oxford English Dictionary

vietnamese word nước means water
vietnamese word nước means country

cháu sống ở nước nào?
child, which country do you live in?
child, which waters do you live in?

an ocean is a stream of water
            water you float in
                        the country you belong to
salts and tans you
            marks *citizen* brown glow

if water equals country,
            and water feeds lives,
                        you survive on country

            therefore water is requisite for country

            therefore water makes country

but here
            a country lies opposite from me
            a country opposite an ocean
            so country opposite water
            a homeland opposite water
            a homeland lying opposite from water is my country

in what nước does this leave me?

I

Natural Melancholia

recall the story   humpback whale's altruism   pectoral fin lifts a diver
who at the surface   filled with a sense of whale's sentience   tells her *i love you too*

here moths land on my abdomen   there monarch butterflies swing   around mountains
no longer in their way   memory passed down   teaches us to ride the wind

my wanting tears slick   my face   a beauty   a sadness   precisely stated
i eat the page and more and   full on Anjou pears   roses and thunder raking the sky

what makes a poet beautiful anyways   tears are a part of my family name   fireflies flit
as i choose fitting clothes for the night   remember the leaping   wings in my stomach

Fifth Grade English

I read the wet pear juice
dripping down the side of its curved line.
Learned to call this word shape—
visual poem.

Later, the afternoon sun
slatted through windows,
and I turned my spiral notebook in circles
wrote a fevered swirl, prepubescent
uncertainty palpitated heart, and
named this shape my own poem.

This the year punctuated, the first
Vietnamese teacher I had (the only)
pronounced my name correctly
even clarified inflections:

Is it Phương or Phượng?

Phương.
So stunned I spoke as reflex.

At recess, against a chain-link fence,
a cracked tennis court no one ever used,
other black-haired children in so many accents
taught me:

thirteen not *tirteen*

library not *liberry.*

Though I still enjoy the hidden fruits in calling it such.
"Thirteen" sits like silt behind my teeth.
My wrong sounds
sweeter, more guttural instinct. Yet,

I read this poem aloud
and remind myself
not to *fill* but *feel*.

What Is (Cannot Be) Left Behind (Ever)

My family di trú
to the states. We moved, we
left behind. We sat
in airplane hull, really
seats with in-flight service.
Lucky not to sail, to sink, to be stolen
by pirates, or worse. We did not leave
crushing with feet the ground,
others' hands, helicopter
pad, streets' rubble,
nor embassy rooftop. We did not
know. Instead,

only took years of hunger,
a little malnutrition, only
took goodbye to grandmother,
village river, pomelo trees; only
required dad's service,
reeducation camp, starvation.
(He tells of prison cells
and catching rats—meal
supplement. Now drinks Ensure
for appetite lost.)

To move forward, one leaves
behind. Or do we?
"Di trú" does not let me forget.
I migrated from this word
and all the ones I could have written.
Feelings convoke connotations,
a gut sense, a poetry lost; and here
I weigh the benefits and wonder if
uneasy gratitude is any at all.

Amputated Remnants

my people believe in land.
roots of every

child embedded in soil—
bloodied placenta and battled star.

watched over by creaking
bamboo, by the emptiness

between tea tree branches,
candelabra arms mossed swords,

green ghost overlords of the cut cord.
aching phantom limbs exist, accentuate

womb that once rocked me, wanting
my earth bond to be ours.

His Own Business

my father rubbed the soft young magnolia leaves.
the trees growing in planters, sentries guarding
steps leading up to the white woman's house.

he landscaped
but by landscape i mean he was a faceless, sweaty gardener
paid in cash. he shaved geometric hedges, cut

grass, repotted bonsai trees, installed ticking
sprinklers, rid every corner of weeds invading.
i imagine he felt he was in his mother's garden—

a grove of tea trees and a perimeter of boxwood.
could have felt like a good son again
who would have stayed and dusted the altar daily.

he would have tended to death anniversaries:
invited men and women clothed in white
gathering to mourn the vietnamese way

around death, a constant we accepted.
any head of the family should have done this,
but here, his back bent over other people's land.

his neck curved over someone else's flowers.
older women with enough money to order him
and he picked through their tasks, thorough

for a reasonable price. he set
his own schedule and spoke as little
english as needed.

he held his tongue but he
held his tongue wrapped around names:
hoa phượng, hoa mai, hoa sen,

under the heavy sun and the up climb
of lawnmower onto pickup truck,
he held his peace, inside.

Dear (Returning) Exile

found poem using words from Mai Der Vang

It's a herd of moth
when my parents left

Calling to my mother
to leave in your bomb
Every minute further   became   a never locket
hanging from the sun

It was good
marbled down
to her lungs kept
closed for you
as stone over the sea

Into old river
floated you to the land
Emptying child years

You my father's face
You crawled back

Relearn cathedral
fly back after winter

Never of plumeria
step back   never a last scent

Horses gaze
reclaim their steppes

It's the Siberian
Ridgeline vista spilling out

The banyan must crane
forbidden of its roots

Folk's Blue Note

a woman who could be my mother
stretches her voice across
the riverboat floating down Perfume River
her head encircled in a frame
of light   gold fabric plays off yellow
flecks of her red silk dress

her pitch wavers   the end
of every line   a blue
note   voices   a grief   song
death wails   over water

now i know   brothers and i   slept to   fell into   wallowed with
sound of heartbreak   lessons

mom hovered   over
swung   our bassinets   hummed the low notes
hung   the swarth of dark

here every song   a folk song
every lullaby   a long linger   a line a lineage

This Is the Dream

in the sun, brown men glow
as i hear the clop of their hammers;
they nail new siding to a building, staple
tar paper to a roof, whack weeds off the edge

of a yard. always these men of soil
and gasoline bring me to my father,
a different brown but brown. i picture
him standing with his friend

by the railroad tracks.
the construction store. a food truck.
they wait to be picked up, to labor the day
forever a bit unsure if the cash will come

from the hands that work them.
years later, opening Dan's Gardening,
dad and i would walk rich
neighborhoods with their tall bushes,

leafy maples, and so much lawn. flyer:
roll blue sheets into handrails or
slip them under welcome
mats. i imagine dad would drive

by Home Depot, point out a few men
he didn't know; then all of them with English
unsteady on their tongues would arrive
somewhere they didn't know,

there, they would bow over rakes, uncertain
about the day's earning. here, i sweat
in the summer heat. wonder if this is
the American Dream—

for my Vietnamese father to fight alongside some,
in a war abandoned, and when they decide
to allow entrance, he earns the right
to cut their grass, build their homes,
reiterate hierarchy and hire.

Home-cooking

like mom i gather gently in palms
amaranth leaves   purple-red stems
green veins   of arrowheads
remind me of her calves
variegated balls of dough protruding
from summer skirts   while she
makes new everything

sssssss says the sautéed shallots
shrimp and pork slices   dress up
boiling broth with leaves
mom bangs pots   until
glimmering deep purple-black broth
grease spot stars
unveils vegetable soup   galaxy

Present Absence

grandmother stands woven somewhere between

silence and languages you speak—wrong tones and mistranslations.

the fine mesh of "you" and cháu.

caught between columns of time

she howls for you. haunting

is another logic. every move

causes vibration. matter and spirit never forget

inscription. written in air

past words breathe in today's spilling

form. she models how to flip

containers   sublimate ties. uncontrollable

overflow. distance touches

everything   and everything cannot be

undone. she broaches a taut string

that wobbles and tangles

all it pretends to divide.

Ode to Sweet Potato Greens

if you forgot   me on soil   under shade
me   left   abandoned   near trash pile
near rotting   i promise   to return

i promise my end   not yet here   not death
not near   i turn inward   pull sweet water
i swear   regeneration   my design

my strength   keeps coming   return is what i know
you have not   grasp(ed) how thick   life lives in the eye
understood   how i will again   how i grow and grow

Am I Welcome to Make Anew

Migrant child says, let me see the lineage
that leads to some soil, womb skin, guava
seed. Rice field, buffalo whip. She becomes new,
of readied mouth and concrete name. Says,
I too am the pulse of basketball on blacktop
after school's out, clean white shoes and a line-up.
This country—and thus we—made of Black hands.
I know Oakland neighborhoods not listed on maps—
Dubbs, Funktown, Ghost Town, Deep East, Seminary.
Like the hands that claim these streets theirs,
another blood runs rivers through me—
delta-colored and city fortress. As newcomer, as faulted,
I have belonged to the music of cars touching
bumpers and the men outside smoking,
the breeze a respite from dinner. Porch culture,
lean-'gainst-the-wall culture, have a cigarette,
do your hair and nails, salon culture.
I am from all this, these places—synthesis of differences.
Contradictions that agitate me. Pull at my skin,
make warm party of ruptured blush.

Migration's Undoing

on a bus watching in reverse—away perpetually—
i move towards a stop not in view.
to gain, one loses landscapes
and i am hurled, moved
by another's progress. i am in motion
therefore i am. someone not
stable
scribbled this. for some, the ground jerks
uncertain. premises shift
and men with papers expect
we stand stoic behind walls. they taunt
images of gold and security gate.
when pushed and lured this way,
movement is not always a choice.

i want to place myself on a vehicle speeding
from anything. to allow hindsight to work,
give transportation time to move me. put me
in my place, so i arrive to an unformed destiny.
tell me my story how it makes sense:
backwards, letter by letter—

Mom Threw a Party

grandma strung army canvas
streamers, fed the fire—
the coals grew ash—laid out
sliced steamed pork,
took our toenails,
sprinkled on lotus root
salad, sent the boy
on loan for a bag
of ice. don't serve
river water. oxen
looked on from fields.
the herons came in
for a peck and auntie picked
smashed fish
herbs, set a plate,
garlic and bird chilies—
sun-shaped for snacking—
spooned out small
bowls of fermented
dirt, leftover
bombs.

I Explain to My Father Again, It's Nurture Not Nature

these are learned obsessions
no warm squeeze

we taught with infinite ocean peaks
held by hands no longer there

we learn this stare infinite too
horizon eyes

learn that wanting and never
arriving are optimal conditions

dream that big
dream you holding grandbaby

but only dream it
i rub my own belly in sleep

maybe my parents avoid touch to practice
us to never miss it

introversion turns inside out
defend against attachment

keep insular   the bigger the circle
the more you lose when you leave

my bag is self-contained and packed
i hear myself the loudest in sadness

like walking out   a feeling echoed

Exception

The most gentle thing is the empty chair
      next to you. A space I could wish in-
to. Today the leaves are wormed with yellow
      against the blue skies' fresh, infested
with a cool, so I think *Fall*—the season
      and the action. This afternoon, oh,
how I imagined a walk with you, since
      being in love makes a poet truly one.
Yet we check our pulses, with our own hands;
      I recall your elsewhere apartment.
When I chose this mountain landscape, could I
      tell how distance would rot, mar itself.
My room here two arm spans wide; too much,
      though I like exceeding, except like this.

Mapping Failures: In Constant Motion

this poem spits in the face of boats,
the waves, the thirst that swallowed
our torsos, the laws, the conferences,
congress sessions bringing us here.
i tear the page to re-make me.

the poem is my anti-map—
all my feelings marked in relation
to no one in space. i
am motion, so are the landmarks.
time circles, so can my sentences
          (that's how i'll tell it).
in the best scenario,
words hurricane—climate
wetter (i must learn there is no way forward
          nowhere to go)
down the interstate of this form. centripetal
stanzas tornado me on a spinning
compass; arrive on the tip
of a distant arrow, trued
to a never destination
          not reached
      in forward
    motion.
  i slant
into the spiraling sun.

A Day's Work

words would arrive to my closed eyes,
and sitting up in bed, i wrote in a yellow
pad. these days, i don't sleep through the night
as well, don't stumble into lines in the dark.
shake myself awake as my body heats for morning.
i had a dream last night. i arranged blue
cornflowers in a bud vase. a poet who looked
like me entered and asked for help. the grape hyacinth
outside calls me. i rise,
stretch my legs into jeans.
visited, i work a bit differently now
for these words laid in order.

II

Other (History of Blue)

This Orientalist Blue, a blues,
the last color of this last
pen of its kind in store but never the last
of this story

Mundane errands find me still colored
blue: covered in decree signatures
indigo pot port agreements
colonial inkwell porcelain treatises
seventeenth parallel

Blue marks land claims and Geneva
Accords. Blue suit
and tie—lawyer assigned
to define death and divide
in your courts. Call me Indochina.
With quick strokes,
pen tube of modernity's ink, your name
scrawled makes a river a border

Who am I to defy the religion of your colors?
Your gods have been making me
centuries before, mapping oceans and charting skies;
collaging nations in explosive tonnage,
you place me on territory outlines
a severed limb at a time.
History in the present,

now I acquiesce, buy
the last pen. Scribble this letter
addressed to my Others, knowing
my face warped, my voice
blued; my ghost
family, they wait for me,
ever blue

In Which Language Burrows

tonight   i look up grief
in my vietnamese-english dictionary

i've given up the dream
of knowing more   in my first language

đau buồn
            means sadness bodied
body resonates sadness
            the wound oozes
unstable   even adjectives move

my loose grip   my grip loosened—

i scramble for this
                this language ledge

my speech an anglo hold   with rocky footing
            in any direction i reach   diacritics slip

here i study
            new weighty connotations
as if at home in my foreignness—

What Is the Angle of a Round Tongue

In Vietnamese, the wrong tilt of tongue says another word sends the speaker to the wrong address and the listener twisting in the litany of possible meanings waiting.

In our Vietnamese, the wrong tilt of tongue mixed with English means the mother and the father get half an idea fill-in-the-blank a stripped canvas.

My brother explains nông trại in a conversation we both agree we have forgotten the surroundings the passing forests but the destination became the word he repeats again and again. Nông trại! Nông trại! because our vocabulary only tells us to raise our voice our mother sits wondering five camps? nam trại? She thinks nông gia? farmer? She arrives close enough to understand his error. Ahh she says—

A raised voice beats down like a slipper slaps but restrains as straitjacket as a cut tongue rising too fat in its skin.

A railroad car out the mouth

production of words stopped short. Choke

how we speak.

Indelible Ink

To be bulletproof
ink is to be smear-
proof. You advertise.

The ink draws caricature. Draws me
apart, pulls at chemical compounds. Just
an outline tossed
aside, left behind. Condition
made solid by paper.

But on me—
flesh of a counterstory—
seawater, all water,
will bleed your ink.

Empty blue washes
over, colors, my body. Blur
border lines. Easy,
I get lifted from the page,
wiped out.

Ocean laps, unmakes
your art project. Illegible
now, pass me over;
I'm a past thing. Absence
I'll take

Diaspora Is No Way Out

memory of mine touted   like tail ends flutter   a way of knowing
basket outside   branches pruned   living as if
the body   torn from self   watching

if time distorted   space too is moved   of course migrant outcome
only option left   deep red scar   is haunting
for mind   disconnection   untethered swing   a wildness circles

family ties thinned   snipped (jagged)   of course migrant release
makes sense then   exits morph   we run   from feeling   embodied
become a wisp   survive anew   is trauma

Legacy / Inheritance / Fortune / Gia tài

after Trịnh Công Sơn

to mong is hoping
while knowing the likelihood

dismal as a horizon always disappearing.

footprints in hard clay soil
while body pressing weight
cannot be seen; aloofness runs

in the family. daughter comes back too late—
sneaking
into acceptance. returning home

means slipping through lines
that won't shade her skin right, that stretch

the road too long, that scar her
with their barb, while mom longs
to hear steps approach,

mistaken for the sound
of her own heart against chest against
rib, *longing.* a word—

to mong—

an endless wish, a strong desire,
face passing in the window.

to trông
to want a face, to summon a body, to wait
and wait

as the only certainty

On Generational Memory

after (and in response to) Ruth Madievsky's "On Memory"

One does not remember the burning
home, but the women who look like our mothers
sliced and penetrated, their scarlet shapes,
smell of barbecue, while a Marine unit scatters.
Remembers not Agent Orange, but the babies'
wails, the golf ball throats and
half a curled limb. Not embargo,
but growling stomachs, mom feeds us
then sobs behind a curtain. Not orphanages,
but metal bars as lilting voices play
ball, bouncing against cement, their echoes
echoing. Not the kill numbers, but the now-dead
brother's words before enlisting, his empty
space in bed, and him, yes—
the killed brother after all.
One recalls details. Not grandma and grandpa,
but the smell of humid concrete to strange grandchildren
returning, dusty packed polyester, and incense
sticks before altar portraits. No, not
grandma and grandpa. No, one forgets.

On Cycle

after Sade Adu

Fan spins turbid, on
and on, thick whirl of air whips
against my legs. Water recycles
through fish tank filter, rapid
forced trickle. Grass outside cut
every week then it shoots
high. Heavy summer thunder
each time cumulonimbus clouds
draw close. The house's stucco
wall warm then cool as night
falls. Round, round, we go. Again,
I am wet in saltwater. Again,
holding something; brick-shaped
tin appears in my hands
the weight of grandmother's heart.
I squint through puffy lids, dutifully
carry my gift, my burden
to the post office, my work bench,
the vanity mirror. Each day,
I could be anywhere—browsing records
in a bin, in the sun-washed street,
to the hair salon, a park—and suddenly
I am with package, this blood slosh.
Avert my eyes from the crowd.
Ignore this rusting box, I tell you;
this container, this cycle
I never chose but would not
change. A quiet becomes unruly
roar in the mundane. It returns
to me. I return to it
until I cannot tell
if I have summoned
my own face.

Cho Ba: A Daughter's Sestina

I imagine you holding up your hand,
rejecting behind the telephone signal wall.
You ask as always about mountain weather;
tell me of rain by the Bay and pause,
wait for me to bridge over water.
I can hear you frown as we part in quiet.

This has become our meeting place, the quiet
where we watch each other; palming hands
turn object of study over and over. I water
your orchids, peppers, and jasmine. Turn wall
into mirror; the other is myself. Pause.
Watch inevitable events as the weather.

I present what reminds me of weather:
your calm humidity, the float of snow, quiet
pool of thought. Mom is a mover, you know pause:
slow lifting and a shovel's wood, callusing hands,
steady as the rain meets sidewalk, side wall,
my face, which you must blur in this water.

I imagine you crossing through water,
fatigued, swimming possibly, fighting weather,
seeking ancestors to dissolve time's wall.
Find those you believe you left in a quiet
tomb and lay beside them. Nothing in hand.
You have bridged, and now may pause.

From the other side, I watch, paused,
uncertain of your direction in water.
I keep this garden built with your hands,
but without you, the flowers wilt; wonder whether
it has rained in forever. You answer in quiet.
I peer at you, pierce through the wave wall

and wonder when I will break this shared wall.
I eye you across ripples; paused
by the distance grown long and quiet,
rumbling. I make up my mind or the water
makes me believe I can overpower weather.
Look at them: consider the potential of my hands.

We have both pushed up walls; both our hands
hovered, paused. Have both fed stormy weather
and this quiet we have believed we inherited like water.

Appellation // Lover's Dare

Appeal to me—call me my name.
Petition for my presence. Your request
a begging desire and lust cannot be recorded.
The stenographer raises his head and wonders
the keys. Say my name and call it
correct. Let the sound rub pass teeth
and see how you need these syllables
in your mouth. I dare you

to want it. The right words
can bring this body there
to you. To know my name is to tug
wrist, subpoena to courthouse.
Prove your claim and receive a ruling,
what we make in seeing each other
in relation, aloud.

To Handle You

How does someone remember a face
across time? No marble carving or oil
portrait for me. Thousands of miles
away I vulture your eyes in circles;

your past inquiries float
to me. Kindness has a life
its own and memory turns
up the volume.

You come to me like flashes,
a fragmented video, disco ghost,
flamboyant spirit. Have I gotten
used to living with phantoms?

How can I build
a future on pictures of ghosts.

No voice on the phone, no
laugh to remind me how air works
its way through your body's
harmonica. No outline of flesh,
these ripples we make into each other.

This is how I want
to handle you, your neck—
the morning's dark mane curling
in my palms. The sun glows through us,
nestled and here.

When Petals Open, They Prepare to Fall

Our sight lines touch, telescope.
I weigh how much you say in this silence,
words you might slip out.
Imagine the language of your body on mine.
Think of the last secrets placed in my ear wells.
I carry them into rotting.

My flesh a colander, catching
enough sentiment to conclude
you will not stay.
I do not search your mouth,
that cavern of disappointment, for feelings.

We know this type of tussle.
You, the man, with his voice and no useful words
and I, destined to thread time through the stars,
forced to enjoy the weaving:
Remember, I am distance-ridden too.

If Language Is a Metaphor Between Sound and Meaning

and language is a metaphor between symbols and meaning,
then, our bodies close feel figurative for other closeness.
I should know you don't like the blinds closed in daytime.
The specks of oil on the stove. I won't ask about your mom, I'll listen.
I know when to tell my story because you are cleaning
the counter, not peppering me with questions. I'll touch
your back in wide sweeps instead of rubbing the skin of your elbow.
You tell me I'm nervous. You make me nervous. While you drive,
I want to rub the succulent of your ear because deep in me
is the metaphor of separation. I keep reaching and you say stop.
I don't know how, but I'll try. If our bodies are not touching,
I may fail to be touched.

In the Canals of Thought

Mass of wires bird's nest of cables power lines above me in Colorado
some gray alley gray building behind a tea house a creek
a two-lane boulevard as American as ash trees deep in August's
frayed feathers where thick black ropes vines branches whatchucallits
like rubber electric tunnels stretched taut across air the mess floating
by someone's balcony three floors up an apartment space to beat the summer heat
like suddenly I am looking up in Sài Gòn Huế somewhere in a balmy alley
white underwear on hangers drying by electric transformer and I
overhear the neighbors chat sitting on short plastic stools sniffing
between chili snot and noodle slurps the basil and beef hanging
in humidity tell-tale signs of any dense place its animal tangle
smells and sidewalk denseness man-made sky-high knots
tightrope for currents under there I stand and I look and I am
teleporting time tripping child of electric vision

Transposed in Traffic

a scooter idles
the sound of hovering
picture it carving

hollow tut-tut
singing ready
through asphalt sea

pulls me aside
to swing into a world
split by yellow glint

like an eel's tail
undulate to evening
life eeks by

weave of red light
bikes dodging blockade
a dribble   there i was

cutting the traffic mass
the slow plug of humans
but know i was not

not there but in a picture
crisp frame of *once*
then i am there

rectangle slot moment
dissociative reaction
memory flip switch

not there   not fully
body a split screen
slide me in

Traversence

What is the speed of light at my desk.

I count to five slowly after a flash of lightning.

A mosquito dies in my notebook. I do not notice when.

There is a light between the pages. There.

Sky, the brightest blue behind the catalpa tree.

Green lit up—a vision of dark stalk and sun-glow leaves.

Rain becomes hail becomes soft rain then—silence.

I am a child in yellow rain jacket hopping across a puddle.

The brain makes electrical connections at the speed of 156 miles per hour.

The speed of a Google algorithm: 2 seconds.

A smell of some old thing in the street transports me in .04 seconds.

My hand reaches out for this tug. In my mind, the hand remains extended.

I time travel too easily.

I ring of repeating names ((((Lai. Đoan Thị Gan. Lê Thị Lạng. Ro.))))

Their beings sum to the ratio of names I do not know.

My grandmother dies and I can never remember her age.

Other times the electrical connections stutter. Obstructed spark plug.

Instead, remember palm leaf's drag on dusty ground.

Remember adolescent re-meeting her.

A cement well in the afternoon, countryside. Sweetness of ripe jackfruit.

Heavy water evaporates quick in the tropical heat to return again.

My grandmother dies and she is always dying.

What is the speed of memory?

The speed at which ancestors travel: _____.

Appellation // Potential

call me and i see arrival
relocate relationship particles
      say the word and   it comes to you
      name the people   and you go to them
letters arrange sentences   compose music
      incantation   teleportation   telephone
      revival   strike   erasure   murder
mis-naming is re-naming
is another way to make something
      yours

i will take back the right
      to air   exit   push   to claim the sounds i speak

i will bless every frightening
      haunt   a label of mine   and
      become the higher court

i will offer you
      all the right
      mispronunciations

there lies honey marrow
in the most gnarled bone   there
is a space for my body
and the appeal that curls in it
      thirsting for room
echoes of all the words   we are worthy
      of imagining

III

Trời Ơi

meaning: *sky, good,*

goodness, heaven, weather

we talk about trời

trời mưa

    the sky is raining

    meaning the weather rains

    meaning the heavens rain

the heavens are good

    the gods up there

    the God up there

    Lord up there

    help us

    trời help us

    sky help!

trời xanh we say

    the sky is blue

    also the sky is green

    goodness green

goodness grief!

assume we know the words

assume the position

assume the meaning

of a sound has not tumbled

say trời ơi!

In My Afterlife, I Am Brightest

after "Untitled (Chauffeur Funeral)," by Daisy Patton

Golden cellophane bows on wreaths, floral
vines transgress the casket's ivory
satin lining. The floor, a jade-colored rug,
covered in bouquets. Purple palms
form a triangle framing the dead. After life,
there is this: proximity of black
lace, a sheer lavender curtain's ruffle. My spirit
rising as rambling branches in this funeral
parlor. I trespass
the composition. I am
beyond. It's true what they say—
enrapt, I watch you from out here. A climbing
rose wraps tighter, determined,
invasive, celebrated. See
how in death, I infiltrate.

Reacquaintances

for grandmother

the way wind breaks through squares

 in window screens, how the glass drains

itself left alone,

 bluebells lean into the brick path. there,

she is there. awaits your eyes.

 you know

the spirits step lightly,

 press shadows on carpet, sweep

through altar plates of full fruit. smoke

 swirl caress when she nears.

holds you between pillowcase palms,

 pulls blankets—just right.

you know

 she watches you cry. the body

of her curves in your tears.

Bà Nội, She Will Rest at Sea

Bà nội, the water rises.

What once worried me was never finding you.

The grass grown high,
a cemetery, a mile-long walk from which direction
I don't know.

My father asks a neighbor, can you help
find my mother's headstone. Another neighbor
shrugs. The sun presses, calls out

sweat. Slip. My back. Curved
shoreline, vertebrae of relative
links. For reasons I have not learned,

the grave is a wide circle.
We find your body's
sphere, wipe the stone, light the stick, bow

with incense.
The dead trace us,
perforated line forever tied, not always

tight. My father wounds the twine. His
secret layers many faces much guilt
seeps. I stand in sun. Water rises.

Familiar Logic

If you can't remember your mother's song, then the green beans cannot be coaxed into growing.

If you don't visit home, then the peeling paint will crumble honey in the corner.

If the ceiling fan's cool pours over you, then your man's thinking of your thighs.

If the singer's metallic gaze slices the room, she drags you in her lips' warble.

If you let go, then ghosts hold tighter, pull the foreground of every family photo.

If mountains, then oceans distant.

Over the phone, your mother sings Vietnamese too fast. So, this is the pace of her love coming for you.

In distance, how close am I to grandparents' haunting. In closeness, a story of our failed intimacies.

Bà nội is over my shoulder, in my hair, urges me to divulge, connect with the eyes of people who raised me too.

The voices keep me tied to names and gardens, of markets and rice, of fish sauce, of rattan corner stores.

If logic worked to explain the dug-out hole, a drop of yellow sun lives forever on your tongue.

Words rise over time, like ghosts of land of humidity of altar smoke. Our family inflates an atmosphere of silence in the throats of fish, gutted mouths, scarlet gums from plankton shards.

A sentence to incorporate the causality of me is weed-whacked by nuance.

Mom's noodles, plus chili oil, plus coriander, then her chest and the couch after dinner. Sitting still holding her is a knowing, deep and lucky. Bright.

What kind of logic is this?

If butterflies on fireweed stalks. If foraged mushrooms smell of pine. If chandeliers of maple samaras.

If a dry leaf on ground lifts dust,

If if if

History as Migrant's Cento

> *But of course, the history of people searching for political asylum*
> *and opportunity (both) is much larger than Eritrean history alone.*
> —Aracelis Girmay

I am There & he
is Here,
      really,
My bones are your bones, he says.
                 Says
if you don't read this, you will turn into birds.
      The rustling of wings
          caught in soil
calling me to repair it.
He asks me to read the mail. Not birds, *mail.*

I needed to say
      you remind me of my father.
                So
Do not go.
      Leaving is a bucket of mosquitoes
         no one empties.
A current. The hands
      of water wave,
          each one waving.

Tiếc

i pick through herbs
green spears of home
leaves i barely take away

spicy Vietnamese coriander
flavor a meal
toss rotted edges

you've coaxed from ground
and i leave the yellow-green
you say don't be tiếc

throw away more
you say don't be so frugal
what is regret here

what's going bad
but tiếc means to regret
holding on to bits

don't be stingy
so wonder what
is to act regretful

tiếc names regret ahead
i would regret it
to save a little more

regret in the subjunctive
would act as if regretful
to stave it away

if i throw this out
we know, i think
the potential of ache

Nhớ Nhiều

my father would doubtless ask
        about weather and i
           would not tell him how
                wet air reminds me
                    of Việt Nam, my missing
our silence, galactic weight
        to bear alone, all of us
           tense as the word love
                a family that reveals might crack
                    or just him, so i owe it
to knuckle tight
        think where in Huế the sidewalk
           can split and i swim
                against the reaching
                    dreams of plumbing and steel
blue as a scarf i feed
        my own mouth as sure as
           sad
                while we keep treading water
                  how i feel tonight
in a plucked zither
        as rain sheets us

Immigrant's Lament

I wish I could tell what's next,
keep the cut lilacs tall a few more days—
just until the peonies bloom. The sun strengthens.
I wander the river walk, my small sphere.
I'll stay folded in myself, promise to memorize
the bramble and texture of garden walls.
Smile on every rodent finding its meal.
Grow magnanimous in quiet's chaos.

Even the hawk strays but swoops,
returns to its treetop to find again
its true nature. Could it be this is mine—
to reach out and hold. From here, wait—

the phone buckles under *I love you's* mass
strung up so you do not hear in time
the words tumbling from my mouth to nowhere,
while they send back all your kind.
All I can do is hold out my hand. You—

I can only imagine you reach back.

A Repeating Distance

I am far from my mother. The distance won't end soon.

My mother is far from her mother. The distance started long ago.

We advance away; each generation replicates

journey, what rhymes with opportunity. Each

tests the tether of ties to what came before,

what it means to come from. Away from a mother,

how many years will undo my making, how many

to make me lose her, to lose an origin,

to change my reply? "Where are you from?"

I'll be asked again and again

and my mouth dries, pulled thin. Brittle from distance,

my smile splinters. If I repeat an answer,

will its meaning change. Will my mouth bleed. Will that blood

remind me who I am from. Will it rest my body

in their long-gone ashes. Does a question fail;

is an answer too simple.

Trịnh Công Sơn's Children

Trịnh Công Sơn's children sing into the navy sky—
each note a bright spot in a dark basin overturned;
each song a new full moon, a spotlight or river,

some reflective thing. Trịnh Công Sơn's children
know the end of the world will split into a poem
to be sung. Know to call a war a silly war if it kills us—

our loves—any of us at all. His children
walk on land far from him; they don't always sing
his words back. But they always carry them still

in the hum of their breath, the purr of a motor
bike, the black-rimmed glasses' tilt,
long cigarette exhales stinging; say

I will đi thăm—a promise—come
and visit them, child of Việt Nam
of yellow skin, who loves her people

as her self. Come with everything
now changed, see your people touched by sun
and grief and market and paddies. Their faces

tan with the salt of their heavy. Trịnh Công Sơn's
children walk through overgrown graves,
grassy cemetery of those spilled on hillsides

left there. His children know about flesh,
its easy deflation. Trịnh Công Sơn's children
wave flags with fading shapes, they

will croon you over a bia, as a lover, by the cool
of the river, will slip a song into your other hand.

What Good Is Silence

On the day I lose my voice
I wade through a park's
clover, grass, and milkweed

I watch a woman tap the spot
to where her dog gallops
and releases his ball

Listen as bike entourage circles
the Lake's perimeter,
a ganging up of joy, a charge
of beats unleashed from speakers

I see in my quiet:
exploded bass blown, exposed
pomegranate arils, a bougainvillea
fuchsia cloud, inverted bomb blast,
infrared ray split, another's speech
spilled from throat

In excess, struggle
to observe sanctity

Silent, I am
apocrypha made sacred

Wordless, I am
not blasted blaspheme

Speak through hips moving
in city—fleshed out and godly;
my eyes touch
others, stoke fires in raised brows

I hear clearer than ever, my prayer
honest as quiet as breath

This meditation to speak
wind-up to strike
more accurate than ever—
yet some will ask
what good is silence?

Những Xác Người Will Not Speak Tonight

I want to do anything but tell you or write this poem. I'd like to walk
to lunch. Sip my tea. Read another translation. Let
the playlist slip into another song. But if my chest is a window,
let there be fog in surgery. Glean what I let you.

Start with anesthesia: I explain the city streets, how they quanh co,
curve like these words and the shapes required of my mouth—
a rounded grave. Remind me of temple's mái hiên, run for cover.

Second, make eight-inch cut in the chest: let me tell you about people
lying bơ vơ—sounds like a kite, they float, firefly, also lay
lonely plank. Bodies scattered bloated syllables.

Then breastplate is broken to expose the heart. Vổng—
even Vietnamese dictionaries do not define for me.

The more I write, the closer I get
to explaining. Connect me to bypass machine,
make hybrid. Here comes the reveal:

I sit up, stab the space between your index finger and thumb—

your xác. This word meaning not just corpse, cut
and dry, but weight—the rind, the peel and core of a body.
Like xác trái cây, it is best to eat fruit whole. While xác người

only has the earth's mouth. Only the rice fields
to feed, transform into hơi for our ride
next year. Must be a way to reach tomorrow.

Now, here, no one can close what has been cracked,
no healthy vein, no bone will meet. Chest open,
trong mưa lạnh, I wonder alone which xác là em tôi?

Between Ridges, Bilingual Burnings

I am still in streams of commas and mountains.
My books will never bridge   the roads to them.

Tectonics of diction here do not include
the pronunciation of my name.

Parents' Bay landscape explodes. Wildfires
hang black veils over Napa homes.

I think of melting washing machines
burning antifreeze and shifting smoke.

Do words even apply? *Mom, buy masks!*
Loud, my tool, emphasis across distance.

Though I am stuck in snow, remember
the words for burn, fire, grasses.

How do I say drought and chemical?
Line breaks   I sound.

She understands my mixed slush;
from the flames   calms her child.

She trusts survival. Explains   roving wildfires
burn more predictable than wars.

Methods for Exodus

after Kaveh Akbar

Pour scalding water on the old.
Roast over a fire until brown.
Bury it in files,
cabinets of closets past.
Throw darts at it. Aim
for the center circle of the ex.
He is no longer anything
but a wound that has eaten itself.
Everyone you love is used
to this bread basket—empty.
You open the picture album
and a bouquet of moths
fly out; dry hydrangea petals
crackle and brush by. There,
there, it will be over.
Pages on the bookshelves
flap open like dead flower
wings rustle. They hold forth
images of cemeteries
and rotted over tulips.
You hand back a hibiscus bloom,
but it wilts on his bedside table
even as you exhale into each other.
Understand
there is nothing
to eat here. To leave
curl into your breath.

Rooting

In my parents' basement sleeps a family
list of names. Whose mom, whose auntie,
great-grandmother has a name. Whose uncle,
which medical condition, the lungs—what? A chart
I scrawled on tracing paper, scrunched
into scroll. As if the past—so transparent—
just as brittle. Recall this tenuous. Fragile. Potential
firewood. Crinkles already ash. Faint pencil fades
further. I dream of rescuing it
next visit, bring family map to light, recorded
rope to hold. In danger of destruction,
I will be towed by these lines and future children, and future children
will know branch and bud, stretch into bright.

Origins and Identity Duplex

These things, they make and make me.
When skirting the topic of Việt Nam, I outline Việt Nam.

When skirting the topic of Việt Nam, I outline Vietnamese.
When thinking I have failed some key principle, I am still Vietnamese.

When thinking I have failed some key principle, I am still me.
Reading culture, as if stained deep by ink.

Reading culture, stained deep by ink.
As if what marks me is wave and water, a washing.

As if what marks me is wave and water, a washing here
then gone or altered, not tattoo nor scar.

No, not tattoo nor scar. More like
sacred bath, mineral soak, like I can choose my becoming.

Out of sacred bath, mineral soak, I choose to be.
Elements I'm full of: what I am made of.

I'm full of it: the things I am of.
They make and re-make me.

Beyond the Twitter Age

On this summer solstice the grove of bamboo
whistles in memory's ear, the head
of a fickle beast. You play with History
on the news feed. The accordion of remembering,
its squeeze and flex, now instant electric archive
with continuous scroll. The mood of telling
wavers in political machine's furnace.
Your ear occupied by the new oral story;
generational wisdom minimized in bite-sized
media circus. Meanwhile,
on a planet in the future, a family hoes land,
plants corn, teaches babies to slow like branches
sway in wind. There is a way to life,
survival not touched by white man's law.
Here, eat the soup I've made from leaves I harvested,
the ones moonlight kissed while you were away.

Say Phuong Thao Vuong

Please, go ahead. Say my name and I'll laugh. Who's backwards now;

where I actually start is a hoard in the clouds—a raven of ghosts.

Say them first, rushing for you. In the middle, an adjective for grounding. Qualifier

to make me not another Phương. My self the faint fragrance framed by father's

wordplay, and then first person comes last. The masses, the herds, their hands,

babies—obviously before me. Say my name right,

know my dead early. Know me as of others:

Vương Thảo Phương.

Grandmother Says: New Theorems

i've been taught of the path forward
i too could have the promise:
big machines of thought, their papers,
stamps and a life of Pepsi,
but your voice
textured as summer
tapped me, told me
we had
options for better
a truer way

in this headstrong pursuit for control
a lined border, a field called colony,
what the soldiers do,
i cannot think, starvation in some years
a blanket
bare protection
we kept losing the little
we had no time, nor
a stretch of land
granddaughter

where our shapes intersect
a story of surviving until we're   alive
portrait as a point with vectors

i watch yams sprout
in uneven patches
leaves spread like fingers thicken soup
nothing is straightforward
i know this as i know

my daughter tended a garden
clipped the bit of raveling greens
a wide area irregular in shade
but it grows
we stay alive so

i cross into you, where i've always lived

Notes

The epigraphs are taken from Sara Ahmed's *Queer Phenomenology: Orientations, Objects, Others* and Jodi Byrd's *Transit of Empire: Indigenous Critiques of Empire.*

page 15: This poem contains images from Ruth Ellen Kocher's gigans in *Goodbye Lyric: The Gigans & Lovely Gun* and conversations in her poetry workshop.

page 16: While considering the term "immigrate" or "migrate" in Vietnamese, I looked up "di trú" in an online dictionary (Vdict.com), which translates the word into "to move, to leave behind, to crush with feet by rubbing." One of the phrases draws from this definition.

page 22: "Dear (Returning) Exile" uses most of the words from Mai Der Vang's poem "Dear Exile" in her collection *Afterland.*

page 46: This poem is inspired by Trịnh Công Sơn's song "Gia Tài Của Mẹ."

page 49: In particular, this poem takes after Sade's "King of Sorrow."

page 70: "History as Migrant's Cento" uses lines from multiple poems by Javier Zamora, Monica Sok, and Aracelis Girmay. The poem's epigraph is from Girmay's *The Black Maria.*

page 75: This poem has lines inspired by Trịnh Công Sơn's song "Tôi Sẽ Đi Thăm" and "Người Con Gái Việt Nam Da Vàng."

page 78: This poem is inspired by Trịnh Công Sơn's song "Bài Ca Dành Cho Những Xác Người."

page 82: "Identity and Origins Duplex" plays with the duplex form invented by Jericho Brown. See *The Tradition.*

page 85: Poems with three columns, which fragment and unfragment, throughout this collection are an invented form inspired by the contrapuntal form, which I draw from Tyehimba Jess's writing. See *leadbelly* in particular. This final poem uses the contrapuntal (dual columns) structure.

Biographical Note

Phuong T. Vuong is a Vietnamese American poet and essayist who cannot stop thinking about language, memory, and migration. She is the author of *The House I Inherit* (Finishing Line, 2019). Her writing has appeared in *American Poetry Review*, *Best American Poetry*, *Kenyon Review Online*, Asian American Writers' Workshop: *The Margins*, and elsewhere. Hailing from Oakland, by way of Hue, Viet Nam, Phuong is currently a PhD student in literature and a James K. Binder Fellow at the University of California, San Diego, situated on unceded Kumeyaay land.